AF521997

FRIENDS STICK TOGETHER

APPRECIATING OUR FRIENDSHIP

A FRIEND

IS ONE WHO LAUGHS AT YOUR JOKES WHEN THEY'RE NOT VERY FUNNY AND SYMPATHIZES WITH YOUR PROBLEMS WHEN THEY'RE NOT VERY SERIOUS.

Hair Club For Dogs

A REAL

FRIEND

STICKS CLOSER

THAN A BROTHER.

The Book of Proverbs

A FRIEND IS ONE WHO KNOWS ALL ABOUT YOU AND STILL LIKES YOU.

Henry O. Dormann

THERE ARE SOME FRIENDS YOU KNOW YOU WILL HAVE FOR THE REST OF YOUR LIFE. YOU'RE WELDED TOGETHER BY LOVE, TRUST, RESPECT, OR LOSS—OR SIMPLE EMBARRASSMENT.

MY FRIEND IS NOT PERFECT—NO MORE THAN I AM—AND SO WE SUIT EACH OTHER ADMIRABLY.

Alexander Smith

YOUR FRIENDSHIP IS BETTER THAN CHOCOLATE!—WELL...ANYWAY, IT'S RIGHT UP THERE!

Julie Sutton

LEARN FROM THE MISTAKES OF OTHERS; YOU DON'T HAVE ENOUGH TIME TO MAKE THEM ALL YOURSELF!

THE NUMBER OF PEOPLE WATCHING YOU IS DIRECTLY PROPORTIONAL TO THE STUPIDITY OF YOUR ACTION.

IT IS ONE OF THE BLESSINGS OF OLD FRIENDS THAT YOU CAN AFFORD TO BE STUPID WITH THEM.

Ralph Waldo Emerson

HOW RARE AND WONDERFUL IS THAT FLASH OF A MOMENT WHEN WE REALIZE WE HAVE DISCOVERED A FRIEND.

William Rotsler

YOU ALWAYS FIND SOMETHING IN THE LAST PLACE YOU LOOK.

A FRIEND IS A PERSON WITH A SNEAKY KNACK OF SAYING GOOD THINGS ABOUT YOU BEHIND YOUR BACK.

I HAVE LEARNED THAT TO BE WITH THOSE I LIKE IS ENOUGH.

Walt Whitman

REAL FRIENDS

ARE THOSE WHO,

WHEN YOU'VE MADE

A FOOL OF YOURSELF,
DON'T FEEL AS
THOUGH YOU'VE DONE
A PERMANENT JOB.

DID I CHOOSE YOU?
DID YOU CHOOSE ME?
AND WHAT DIFFERENCE
DOES IT MAKE?
ALL THAT REALLY
MATTERS, FRIEND,
IS THAT WE CHOSE
TOGETHER.

Lois Wyse

A TRUE FRIEND IS ONE WHO IS CONCERNED ABOUT WHAT WE ARE BECOMING, WHO SEES BEYOND THE PRESENT RELATIONSHIP, AND CARES DEEPLY ABOUT US AS A WHOLE PERSON.

Gloria Gaither

WE HAVE BEEN FRIENDS TOGETHER IN SUNSHINE AND IN SHADE.

Caroline E. S. Norton

TAKE A RISK. OPEN YOUR HEART. FIND A REAL FRIEND AND GROW TOGETHER.

Sheila Wals

A FRIEND CAN TELL YOU THINGS YOU DON'T WANT TO TELL YOURSELF.

Francis Ward Wheele

THE REAL SECRET OF HAPPINESS IS NOT WHAT YOU GIVE OR WHAT YOU RECEIVE; IT'S WHAT YOU SHARE.

HAPPINESS IS MY FRIEND'S HAND.

Gillian Queen, age 10

THERE ARE MOMENTS WHEN EVERYTHING GOES WELL, BUT DON'T BE FRIGHTENED, IT WON'T LAST.

Jules Renard

IF YOU HAVE TO START OVER, HAVE A FRIEND BY YOUR SIDE.

Mikey's Funnies

"STAY" IS A CHARMING WORD IN A FRIEND'S VOCABULARY.

Amos Bronson Alcott

THE BEST RULE OF FRIENDSHIP IS TO KEEP YOUR HEART A LITTLE SOFTER THAN YOUR HEAD.

Push One For El Nino

THANK GOD

FOR SPEED DIAL—

I NEED YOU

RIGHT NOW!

HAPPINESS IS A FRIEND WHO PULLS THE TOILET PAPER OFF YOUR SHOE BEFORE YOU MAKE A GRAND ENTRANCE.

GOD GAVE ME FRIENDS SO I WOULDN'T HAVE TO LAUGH ALONE.

WHEN OTHERS ARE HAPPY, BE HAPPY WITH THEM.

The Book of Romans

LAUGHTER IS THE SHORTEST DISTANCE BETWEEN TWO PEOPLE.

Victor Borge

MAN DOES NOT LIVE BY WORDS ALONE, DESPITE THE FACT THAT SOMETIMES HE HAS TO EAT THEM.

Adlai Stevenson

A CLOSED MOUTH GATHERS NO FEET.

THERE'S NOTHING WRONG WITH HAVING NOTHING TO SAY, AS LONG AS YOU DON'T SAY IT OUT LOUD.

SMILE, IT MAKES PEOPLE WONDER WHAT YOU ARE THINKING.

THE PROPER OFFICE OF A FRIEND IS TO SIDE WITH YOU WHEN YOU ARE WRONG. NEARLY ANYBODY WILL SIDE WITH YOU WHEN YOU ARE IN THE RIGHT.

Mark Twain

GENUINE FRIENDS CAN ENTER OUR CELEBRATION WITH AS MUCH OR MORE ENTHUSIASM AS THEY WOULD HAVE IF IT HAD HAPPENED TO THEM.

Lloyd John Ogilvie

FRIENDSHIPS MULTIPLY JOYS AND DIVIDE GRIEFS.

Henry George Bohn

From Sir With Love

A GOOD

FRIEND PUTS UP WITH YOUR WORST MOODS, GOES ALONG WITH YOUR WORST IDEAS, AND ALWAYS SEES THE BEST IN YOU.

GOOD JUDGMENT COMES FROM EXPERIENCE; AND EXPERIENCE, WELL, THAT COMES FROM BAD JUDGMENT.

IN SPITE OF THE COST OF LIVING, IT'S STILL POPULAR.

Kathleen Norris

THERE IS NO PLEASURE IN HAVING NOTHING TO DO; THE FUN IS IN HAVING LOTS TO DO AND NOT DOING IT.

Mary Little

FRIENDS FIND THE SWEETEST SENSE OF HAPPINESS COMES FROM SIMPLY BEING TOGETHER.

LAUGHING AT OURSELVES AS WELL AS WITH EACH OTHER GIVES A SURPRISING SENSE OF TOGETHERNESS.

Hazel C. Lee

LAUGH AT YOURSELF, BEFORE ANYONE ELSE CAN.

Elsa Maxwel

BETTER TO REMAIN SILENT AND BE THOUGHT A FOOL THAN TO SPEAK OUT AND REMOVE ALL DOUBT.

Abraham Lincoln

IF YOU CAN'T GET PEOPLE TO LISTEN TO YOU ANY OTHER WAY, TELL THEM IT'S CONFIDENTIAL.

Farmer's Digest

A FRIEND OF MINE ONCE SENT ME A POSTCARD WITH A PICTURE OF THE ENTIRE PLANET EARTH TAKEN FROM SPACE. ON THE BACK IT SAID, "WISH YOU WERE HERE."

Steven Wright

ALL FRIENDS ARE NOT FOR LIFE, BUT IF YOU HAVE A TRUE FRIEND, YOU HAVE A LIFE.

Lois Wyse

TRUE BLUE FRIENDS... MAKE YOU FEEL GOOD AND WARM.

Adelaide Bry

Big Loud Screaming Blonde

THE ESSENCE

OF TRUE FRIENDSHIP IS TO MAKE ALLOWANCE FOR ANOTHER'S LITTLE LAPSES.

David Storey

I'VE LEARNED THAT YOU CAN GET BY ON CHARM FOR ABOUT FIFTEEN MINUTES. AFTER THAT, YOU'D BETTER KNOW SOMETHING.

FRIENDSHIP IS THE RESULT OF MAKING A GOOD IMPRESSION LAST.

FRIENDSHIPS ARE GLUED TOGETHER WITH LITTLE KINDNESSES.

Mercia Tweedale

RECALL IT AS OFTEN AS YOU WISH, A HAPPY MEMORY NEVER WEARS OUT.

Libbie Fudim

FRIENDSHIP IS OF SO SWEET AND STEADY AND LOYAL AND ENDURING A NATURE THAT IT WILL LAST THROUGH A WHOLE LIFETIME, IF NOT ASKED TO LEND MONEY.

Mark Twain

THE NEXT TIME YOU'RE FEELING DOWN, THINK OF ALL THE TERRIBLE THINGS THAT DIDN'T HAPPEN TO YOU.

Barbara Johnson

OUR FRIENDS KNOW THE WORST ABOUT US BUT REFUSE TO BELIEVE IT.

FRIENDS...LIFT OUR SPIRITS, KEEP US HONEST, STICK WITH US WHEN TIMES ARE TOUGH, AND MAKE MUNDANE TASKS ENJOYABLE. NO WONDER WE WANT TO MAKE FRIENDS.

Em Griffin

A FRIEND IS A PERSON WHO WILL HELP YOU FOLD YOUR UNDERWEAR.

NOBODY REALIZES THAT SOME PEOPLE EXPEND TREMENDOUS ENERGY MERELY TO BE NORMAL.

Albert Camus

IF IGNORANCE IS BLISS, WHY AREN'T MORE PEOPLE HAPPY?

FRIENDS
FORGET YOUR
DEFECTS,
AND IF
THEY ARE
VERY FOND
OF YOU,
THEY DON'T
SEE ANY.

Don't Look Now

FRIENDS ARE THOSE
SPECIAL PEOPLE
YOU CAN ENJOY JUST
DOING NOTHING WITH...
AND I'M ALWAYS LOOKING
FOR A GOOD EXCUSE TO
DO NOTHING!

Julie Sutton

A CHEERFUL FRIEND IS LIKE A SUNNY DAY, WHICH SHEDS ITS BRIGHTNESS ON ALL AROUND.

John Lubbock

WHEN JUST BEING TOGETHER IS MORE IMPORTANT THAN WHAT WE DO, YOU ARE WITH A FRIEND.

I THINK I NEED A HUG...AND A MAID AND A COOK AND A CHAUFFEUR AND A SECRETARY AND AN ACCOUNTANT...AND A LOT MORE HUGS.

FRIENDS ARE NECESSARY TO A HAPPY LIFE.

Harry Emerson Fosdick

KINDNESS CONSISTS IN LOVING PEOPLE MORE THAN THEY DESERVE.

Joseph Joubert

WE DO NOT REMEMBER DAYS, WE REMEMBER MOMENTS. MAKE MOMENTS WORTH REMEMBERING.

THE TROUBLE WITH BEING AN OPTIMIST IS THAT PEOPLE THINK YOU DON'T KNOW WHAT'S GOING ON.

SUNSHINE IS A MATTER OF ATTITUDE.

F. W. Boreham

GOOD FRIENDS ARE GOOD FOR YOUR HEALTH.

Dr. Irwin Sarason

THE GOOD THING ABOUT OLD FRIENDS IS THAT WHEN YOU'RE IN THE DOG HOUSE, THEY'LL COME VISIT YOU THERE.

Snapped

IF I CAN BE

OF ANY HELP, YOU'RE IN WORSE TROUBLE THAN I THOUGHT.

THE JOURNEY OF A THOUSAND MILES BEGINS WITH A BROKEN FAN BELT AND A LEAKY TIRE.

EVERYTHING I DO IS TWICE AS NICE WITH YOU!

OUR BEST FRIENDS ARE THE ONES WHO PACK EASILY AND TRAVEL WELL ON THE ROAD OF LIFE.

Lois Wyse

CHEERFULNESS IS THE HABIT OF LOOKING AT THE GOOD SIDE OF THINGS.

W. B. Ullanthorne

IF I WERE TO MAKE A SOLEMN SPEECH IN PRAISE OF YOU, IN GRATITUDE, IN DEEP AFFECTION, YOU WOULD TURN AN ALARMING SHADE OF CRIMSON AND TRY TO ESCAPE. SO I WON'T. TAKE IT ALL AS SAID.

Marion Garretty

DO NOT ALLOW GRASS TO GROW ON THE ROAD OF FRIENDSHIP.

Madame Geoffrin

A FRIEND LOVES AT ALL TIMES.

The Book of Proverbs

THE HUMAN BODY WAS WISELY DESIGNED SO THAT WE CAN NEITHER PAT OUR OWN BACKS NOR KICK OURSELVES TOO EASILY.

IT IS OF IMMENSE IMPORTANCE TO LEARN TO LAUGH AT OURSELVES.

Katherine Mansfield

A FRIEND IS A PERSON
WITH WHOM
I MAY BE SINCERE,
BEFORE WHOM
I MAY THINK OUT LOUD.

Ralph Waldo Emerson

GIVE WHAT YOU HAVE.
TO SOMEONE IT MAY BE
BETTER THAN YOU DARE
TO THINK.

Longfellow

To Every Dog There Is A Season: Winter

FRIENDSHIP

IS A COZY
SHELTER FROM
LIFE'S
RAINY DAYS.

FRIENDS STICK TOGETHER

APPRECIATING OUR FRIENDSHIP

Bright, expressive paintings by Tom Everhart, the only artist authorized by Charles Schulz to illustrate Peanuts characters, are paired with lighthearted, fun-loving sentiments in this celebration of friendship.

Design by Lecy Design

Published by Garborg's, LLC
P. O. Box 20132, Bloomington, MN 55420

ISBN 1-58375-466-0

Printed in Mexico